READING
An Essay

BY
HUGH WALPOLE

New York and London
HARPER & BROTHERS
1927

D1248250

READING
An Essay

CHAPTER ONE

READING FOR FUN

IT would be flattering to my intelligence were I able to make this Essay a learned and analytical description of any reader's proper mental processes. I have seen such books, books that point out so clearheadedly what must be read at eight, eighteen, twenty-eight, with careful lists of the fifty best volumes, and cold and impassive descriptions of the world's most famous writers.

Such books must do a great deal of good; we are all so sadly confused and muddle-headed, there is so much to read and so little time in which to do the reading, it is terrible to consider the helter-skelter fashion in which we scurry through life.

Yes, that is the kind of book that I should like to write, and, perhaps, one day I will, but when the time comes for it I shall, I hope, be dried up and withered so that there will be no chance at all of my putting anything personal into it, of my saying that "this time I remember when I was sitting under a green tree on a Spring morning I opened WINTERSLOW for the first time," or "I recollect that the fire was crackling and the snow falling thickly outside as I read the last words of MONTE CRISTO there in the old house near Keswick."

No, in such a book there would be nothing of that kind, only a list of the best authors to be read at eighteen—

    I THE BIBLE

    II MILTON'S PARADISE LOST

    III PLEASURES OF LIFE

    IV THE TALMUD

and so on, and so on. But as this Essay is to be concerned, I believe, with the pleasures of Reading it can be nothing if it is not autobiographical, for the only certain thing about Reading is that it is personal first, personal second, and personal all the time, and Milton's PARADISE LOST and Dante's DIVINA COMEDIA may be the twin dominating peaks of a glorious range, but they are nothing to you whatever if you happen to be looking the other way.

Then this Essay is concerned with Reading and not with criticism. It is a fine and splendid thing to have a critical mind so long as it doesn't take you so far that you can see nothing on every side of you for dust and ashes; the fact remains, however, that on looking around you it is the books that you have loved that count, not the books that you have criticised, and by that, of course, I do not mean that you should be one of those sentimental readers to whom a book is a sort of meringue; readers who wallow in books like pigs in a trough, who read to obtain every sort of emotion save only the intellectual one. No masterpiece has ever yet appeared in the world that can escape criticism; a book is not like a well-made box, so truly constructed that it will fulfill every charge made upon it; a book is a fluid, moving, uncertain thing that is glorious one moment and foolish the next, richly covered here and naked to all the winds there, so clearly intimate at this moment that your dearest friend is nothing to you and so stiffly distant at the next that you wonder whether you dare raise your hat to it.

Yes, that is what every reader who is a reader cares for, this creative ecstasy stirred by his soul in the reading so that there pass before his eyes a few lines of print and in an instant of time he is with Uncle Toby and Widow Wadman in their sacred arbour, walking with Hazlitt on a highroad towards evening, kicking his heels on the hill-top with Parson Adams or plunging into the reek of Dame Quickley's Public in search of Bardolph.

It is an impression of something of this ecstasy that I should wish to stamp into these pages.

To begin at the beginning then, the first book in the world from which I am conscious of receiving any sort of ecstasy was one entitled LOTTIE'S VISIT TO GRAND-MAMMA. From the early pages of it I was first taught to read, and the beginnings were anything but ecstatic. Looking now at the volume I perceive that the first page is divided off (I suppose by the careful hand of my governess) into two lines at a time, and I gather that two lines a day were as much as I could just then manage.

I fancy also from marks upon the page that battles of blood and tears were fought over every word, and one word of three syllables is underlined with desperate emphasis as though here was an obstacle never to be surmounted. So I struggled, I dare say for months and months, and then suddenly liberation came and I paced ahead. I can remember exactly the moment at which my first consciousness of ecstasy arrived. Lottie and her little friend had been permitted by their Grandmamma to go for a walk on the beach while a gale was blowing; there is a picture of them clutching their funny little straw hats, their short spindle legs wabbling below them, and then suddenly an old gentleman's umbrella is blown away and Lottie and her little friend, being not modern children at all, but always rather on the watch for succoring the aged and doing good to invalids, rush after, and in spite of a terrific battle with the gale, secure it for the old gentleman, who thanks them in the most courtly and early-Victorian manner.

I can remember very vividly indeed that this dramatic passage was a revelation to me. I saw it all so sharply that there was no need for the charming picture. My own personal life was instantly doubled, no passages that I read afterwards, whether in the pages of Marryat, of Melville, or of Conrad, gave me more vividly the impression of the perils of the sea than did these few lines; the windows were opened and I knew once and for all what Reading could do for one.

I plunged straight from LOTTIE into the two ALICES, and here was my first impression of a new world. I believed of course implicitly every word that I read, and if you had told me at that time that little girls didn't plunge down rabbit-holes, that rabbits seldom wore white gloves and that mock turtles did not shed tears, I would have laughed in your face. A good deal has been written, I believe, about the logical sequence of the ALICES, about its careful construction and about the inevitability of its nonsense, but I have never seen anywhere sufficient emphasis laid upon the greatest of its powers, namely, the extraordinary resemblance of the figures in it to a child's everyday relations. A child of six or seven sees its elders as "trees walking," their grotesqueness in contrast with the realism of the child's own life is a thing that they happily are unaware of, but a child has many secret chuckles at their incredible absurdities. ALICE was exactly the bridge that I needed; we had a cook so like the Duchess's cook that there was no difference worth mentioning; two of my closest relations exactly resembled the Mock Turtle and the Red Queen, and the mistress of my kindergarten was a positive image of Father William. These resemblances did not strike me as in any way odd; it simply was that the people in ALICE behaved more normally and more reasonably than the people at home.

I felt, however, I am sorry to say, a persistent irritation with Alice herself. I have been a heretic about her all my life, and it seems to me that in her Lewis Carroll was a little talking down to his enchanted audience. I relished from the first all Alice's misadventures, but she was stupider, I felt, than I would myself have been, and I began then what has ever since been a great pleasure to me, a gentle practice of altering events according to my autocratic will. I left Alice, for in-

7

stance, drowning in the pool a good deal longer than Lewis Carroll left her; she bumped her head against the ceiling with a sharper and more painful bump than Lewis Carroll permitted her, and her head was chopped off once or twice by the Queen, just to teach her not to be quite so superior and not to ask quite so many questions.

But the great thing that the book did for me was for the first time to give me another world to play in. I had not at that period a very amusing world of my own; it was constantly restricted, inhibitions abounded and almost everything that one liked was bad either for one's stomach or one's morals. But the morality of Alice's world was supremely satisfactory; I wonder indeed on looking back that the older readers of that time did not object to its laxity. Nobody was punished because of wrong-doing; when anyone suffered it was in consequence of somebody's whim and the suffering never lasted very long; even the Mock Turtle rather enjoyed his tears. The one harassing and eternally distressing episode was the fate of the Oysters; how many versions of that

8

I indulged in for my own tender benefit!
The Walrus became to me indeed the true
figure of sin, and I think that it is from
that time that I date my slight disquiet-
ing disapproval of gentlemen with droop-
ing moustaches. I created a glorious
finale in which the Oysters led the Walrus
and the Carpenter ever further and further
into a sandy desert, standing always a
little out of their reach and watching
finally with enormous glee these two hoary
sinners succumbing to agonizing hunger.
On the other hand I conceived a love for
the Lion who was a friend of the Unicorn;
it was so passionate that I think Ten-
niel's picture of him must have been re-
sponsible for it. There is surely the
dearest and most benevolent of all the
lions, and I remember still very vividly my
pleasure when, on being taken to the Zoo
for the first time, I found a real lion there
to resemble very closely indeed in benig-
nancy and apparent tenderness the lion of
my early love.

It is at this point, when the first discovery has been made of the possibilities of
the new inexhaustible world that children
divide into the two eternal divisions of

mankind, call them what you will, Romantics and Realists, Prosists (if I may coin
that word) and Poets, Business Men and
Dreamers, Travellers and Stay-at-Homes,
Exiles and Prosperous Citizens. Reading
shows which way a child is going more
clearly than anything else in the world.
I fancy that all the children of my day who
gloried in Henty were the Realists and
Hans Andersen was for the others. Henty,
you will remember, dealt always most
severely in facts and however romantic
his adventurous young hero might be on
the first page, the remainder of his pages
stuck so closely to history that it read
like a contemporary newspaper report.
I am not saying that the Henty books
were any the worse for that, but I think,
if my memory is accurate, the little boys
my contemporaries who enjoyed Henty
also burrowed their noses deeply into
strange volumes named THE BOY'S
MECHANIC, THE YOUNG ENGINEER, and
the like.

I could never abide anything that had
to do with facts as such; I am the worse
novelist to-day because of it, I doubt not,
but Hans Andersen's story of the little

tin soldier was worth all the Young Mechanics in the world to me and yet is. I came straight to Hans Andersen from ALICE, and I read him in a glorious, stumpy, green little volume with odd crooked wood-cuts of storks standing on one leg, house roofs thick with snow and nights full of stars. But I doubt whether most children, poets or no, care as deeply for fairy stories as they are supposed to do; there are, of course, a few incomparable ones—RED RIDING HOOD, CINDERELLA, JACK AND THE BEANSTALK, and HANSEL AND GRETEL, and it is interesting to notice that the charm for children in these stories lies very largely in their cruelty, the wolf devouring the Grandmother, the ugly sisters persecuting Cinderella, the terrible ogre at the top of the beanstalk with his victims, the old witch and her boiling kettle.

I was not myself, I think, an especially cruel little boy, being for the most part timid and sycophantic, but from the very earliest age it gave me pleasure to hear of others in distress, because it made my own misfortunes seem less terrible, and this pleasure in the misfortunes of others is one of the earliest self-gratifications we obtain from Reading.

I wonder how long most children remain in the fairy-tale period; in these modern days the time is very short, I should imagine. I remained in it in its simplest form for the briefest moment; I seem on looking back to have tumbled straight from Alice and Hans Andersen into a kind of syrup of romance. Here I must be for a moment even more nakedly autobiographical, because I believe that the reading of every romantic child from the age of, say, nine to thirteen depends so largely upon the atmosphere in which he is living. It *is* atmosphere altogether, nothing is consciously done by the child, but rather the books grow out of the walls of the room in which the child lives like patterns on the wall-paper, or hang from trees in the garden like shining fruit, or swim like gold fish in the bowl in the dining-room window. When a child has a very happy childhood and is surrounded by elders who are showering gifts and benedictions, when the air is filled with light and sun and health and everybody is prosperous and successful, books are not needed; they come as a kind of extra pleasure, things to be looked for when one is tired of everything else, things rather to be patronized.

My own life between those years happened, through no fault of anybody's, to be lonely and dismal and filled with alarums and excursions. I seemed suddenly to grow old; the Hentys and the Grimms and the others were not enough for me, but the VANITY FAIRS and the BARNABY RUDGES (I remember especially trying VANITY FAIR in a state of rebellion after what I thought was unjust punishment) were as yet too much for me. We lived at that time in an old dusty, crooked town whose streets were forever going uphill; I was left a great deal to my own devices, and having on one occasion just before Christmas a penny to spend I determined to buy a book. I had never quite independently of my own account bought a book before; I didn't think it would be difficult to buy a book for a penny; a penny seemed to me a good deal of money. I went into the shop and asked what book I might have for a penny. The

13

bookseller smiled and put in front of me
a pile of thin little books bound in yellow
paper. I can smell still the odd scent of
those books, something musty like straw
and pungent like cheese. I looked at
them one after another and said that what
I wanted was a story. I was quite clear
that poetry would not do. The bookseller strongly recommended one, but when
I found that it was written by the man
whose works had already made two holidays miserable by their compulsory com-
panionship I shook my head. However,
he almost forced it upon me and refused,
I am happy now to remember, to take my
penny. I took it home and that night,
by the light of a guttering candle, began
to read. At first there were difficulties;
the print was atrocious, very small and
irregular, dark at one moment, faint at
the other, and there were parallel columns
to every page. But I struggled on; there
was a curious sense of adventure connected
with the affair; I had bought, or had at
least tried to buy, this book with my very
own money; the silence of the house all
around me, the leaping flame of the candle,
the cheesy smell of the brown cover, even

the very smallness of the print excited me;
this was a new experience. And when I
had persevered sufficiently I came to the
scene in that book which tells of a mysterious chapel and an ugly dwarf and a
kneeling knight therein; a procession of
beautiful ladies enters, and one of them,
surely the most beautiful of them all, drops
a rose at the feet of the kneeling knight.
That was enough for me; that scene prom-
ised me that for the rest of my days there
should be always at my hand a land of
escape and enchantment. I suspect that
the first book to do this great service to
one is very largely a matter of chance;
I can imagine myself, a pale spectacled
infant, absorbed by the wonders of
Smiles' SELF HELP at just this time if
the right kind of uncle, a very serious,
lofty-minded man who had considerable
influence over me, had been staying with
us, or the works of Charlotte Mary Yonge,
works that did, in fact, give me a great
deal of rather tearful happiness, might
have dominated my existence forever had
an adorable aunt who was as generous-
hearted as she was minute been my that-
time hostess. Books, I have already said,

are at the beginning like fruits on a tree, almost all of them so inevitable, so bright and so shining, that the first to fall into one's mouth is, nine times out of ten, the overwhelmingly important one. This, be it understood, always with that recognition of the division between the Romantics and the Realists that I have already mentioned.

I shall have more to say about Scott in a moment, and as a matter of fact I did not at once plunge into the stream of the Waverleys; I fastened on to lesser gods. There was a gentleman called Marion Crawford (is he now altogether forgotten? I trust not) and, with sixpence now in my pocket, I purchased one day a thin volume with a red cover, lured to it simply by its entrancing title, SARACINESCA. Was there ever a more beautiful-sounding title in the world? And for myself at least that lovely name was justified, for I found between those red covers a group of men and women as gallant and stately and courteous as were any of the figures in THE TALISMAN, and they belonged, marvellous to relate, to one's own time. I might find any day just such superb beings in the streets of my own crooked lit-

tle town. Judged by more mature stand-
ards, these figures were perhaps just a
little too superb and stately, but that did
not bother me then; I lived for months in
that fine Italian world, where the women
moved so beautifully out of their dark
sombre houses on their way to the con-
fessional and the men fought duels with
silent indifference that, to my young and
uncontrolled habit of mind, seemed the
perfection of conduct. Let me for an
instant recall their names—Saracinesca,
Sant' Ilario, Don Orsino, Corleone; are
they not exquisitely rhythmical?

And it was through these beautiful romances that I made a yet more thrilling
discovery, namely, the dark, spidery,
musty-aired library which was to give me
many more hours of ravishing enchantment than I can possibly now recall.

Here, I suppose, should come that
eternal question as to whether a child of
tender years should be flung headlong into
the whirlpool of books or no. I don't
know that nowadays the question is any
longer urgent, children are so modern,
have so much liberty, seem to know so
clearly what they want that they read

what they please, I suppose. But when I
was young, thirty years ago, there were
the strongest views about this; certain
books only must be read on Sunday and
many books, of course, not at all, and it
must have been just at this time that an
aunt of mine discovered me with a cheap
edition of Ouida's UNDER TWO FLAGS
and burnt it publicly before the assembled
family, afterwards restoring to me very
ceremoniously the sixpence that I had
spent upon it. Long years afterwards,
when I had been browsing with complete
freedom in this library of mine, I was
scolded for peeping into JANE EYRE, a
book that I had, as a matter of fact, read
from cover to cover long before. That
was the way things were thirty years ago,
but although I think that the library did
no harm at all to my morals, it did dam-
age me, perhaps, in another way—I read
so fast and so furiously that I never
stopped to think about what I had been
reading. At the moment of freedom from
school I plunged down side streets to the
library, left the three volumes that I had
borrowed a day or two before, climbed a
wabbling ladder to the dark mysteries be-

neath the ceiling, and had a glorious dirty half hour of choosing and rejecting.

It was a queer enough place. Its only daily point of vitality was at a small table in the centre of a room where reposed a dozen or so of the more recent books. For the town subscribers to the library this was the only interesting spot in the room, for the lady librarian also. She was a dark, heavy, pale-faced woman whose shadow will forever hover, I fancy, around the memory of all the marvellous books that I read at that time. I am perhaps to-day the human being in all the world who has the most vivid picture of her. She played a fine game at that table, a game of allotting and depriving, a snobbish game, I fear, of keeping the best books for the best people. She would sit upon a choice new volume rather than deliver it over into the hands of some one socially unworthy of it. These were the days of the early Barries, of Crockett and Weyman and Mrs. Humphry Ward, simple days they must seem to our sophisticated modern reader who enjoys his James Joyce and Virginia Woolf. It is a proud thought for the modern day to think that

this good librarian, were she now en-
throned behind that little table, would be
sitting on ULYSSES instead of MARCELLA.

That table meant little or nothing to
me; I was gloriously balanced on the uncertain ladder shaking dust from the
bodies of Bage and Ferrier, Godwin and
Henry Mackenzie, Eugène Sue (I read the
whole of THE WANDERING JEW in a week)
and G. P. R. James. I had no guide to
any of these things; I had at this time
read no books of literary criticism, I had
no notion of anyone's dates or characteristics or personal histories, I simply nuzzled and nuzzled and chewed and chewed.
I have said already that the danger of this
proceeding was that I never stopped to
think. I found FRANKENSTEIN and A
FOOL OF QUALITY and THE ROMANCE OF
THE FOREST (Heaven's blessings on Mrs.
Radcliffe) and SYDNEY BIDDULPH all
equally good and splendid. The dust hov-
ered in clouds about my devoted head, the
ladder quivered and quivered again as
though with sympathetic agitation at my
ecstasies, the Canons and the Canons'
wives came in, fought their battles over
the newer books and retreated, the after-

noon passed and the night wore on, and just before closing time I would be seen emerging surreptitiously as though I had committed some crime, my face grimed, my school cap awry, and DESTINY in three stout volumes under my arm.

I don't know, in fact, at what period in a reader's life the critical faculty should begin to have its sway. I have headed this section of my Essay READING FOR FUN simply because the critical faculty during this period had no sway at all. There is, of course, fun in being critical, some of the best fun in the world, but it is fun that comes later on, I fancy, when that first youthful confidence in an author's infallibility has wistfully passed away. Although I was now fourteen or fifteen years of age books still seemed to grow like bright fruit on trees. If a reader has a fine mind he will, I imagine, very early in his reading history perceive the essential difference between, say, PRIDE AND PREJUDICE and INHERITANCE or between THE ANTIQUARY and ANNALS OF THE PARISH. The truly critical reader begins his business from the very first, discriminating, for instance, between the first

ALICE and the second, and if he has that kind of reading mind he must lose some of that trusting enjoyment that goes with the other kind of reading. On the other hand, the trouble with the ecstatic reader is that he continues ecstatic in all probability until the end of his days, and there is something not a little foolish about an ecstatic, uncritical old man. There are some splendid persons, of course—Professor Saintsbury is a marvellous example of them—who, throughout their lives, keep both their ecstasy and their critical judgment running side by side, but ordinary mortals must for the most part make their choice. In that dusty, dishevelled library I once and for all made mine.

To every reader just at this time there comes, I think, some dominating influence, and this solves, partly, the question as to whether he will be in later life an æsthetic or unæsthetic reader. In the main, of course, because every reader who is the real thing has an appreciation for all sorts, Beaudelaire as well as Hugo, Schiller as well as Goethe, Smollett as well as Henry James. But the dominating influence is what finally tells; mine was Walter Scott.

It is the fashion now, I know, to sneer at Scott, to declare him unread and unreadable, to laugh at his anachronisms, to be appalled by his cumbrous sentences, to shudder before his simpering heroes, to be aghast at his material view. These things run in cycles; we are just now all for sophistication, for technique and arrangement and for a proper dignity in letters, but some day some one will come along who will clear away a little of the clambering ivy and the twisting weeds that have grown thick about the stones of that splendid old building. An enormous amount of critical self-satisfied *cliché* has to be thrown away, and then with a new view there will be astonishment, I fancy, for a good many people.

As I have already said, I had at the beginning to fight against that accursed habit of giving Waverley novels to helpless small boys as holiday tasks, and even after my magnificent discovery of THE TALISMAN I did not immediately pursue the adventure. It was during a Christmas holiday in a Cornish rectory where I was left a great deal to my own devices that I discovered once and for all that row of red, dumpy volumes with the white labels and the steel plates (the only true edition for any Scott lover), and so, taking them one after another into an attic thick with the smell of apples and its windows spider-webbed, plunged headlong.

Because I had an uncritical mind none of it was dreary to me. From the long introductory chapters in WAVERLEY to the halting pathetic last pages of CASTLE DANGEROUS I gloried in every word. It is true that I stumbled over some of the introductory prefaces with their long Scotch words and their curiously named doctors, pedants and schoolmasters, but the very cloudy mystification of these pages enchanted me. The stories when they emerged seemed to come, as they should do, from dark and musty chambers rather like the old library that I have already described. At first the English historical novels, IVANHOE, KENILWORTH and the rest, were the most absorbing, but soon, like every true Scott lover, the Scotch novels led all the others. Only the last chapters of THE HEART OF MID-LOTHIAN irritated me, and I learnt to hold my hand at Jeanie's return from London and leave the rest unread. It was the exuberance of it all, I think, that caused my completest capture; character sprang out of the ground on every side of one, and the smallest, most insignificant figure had only to appear and suggest in a few spoken words or a description of a line or two an infinite vitality. Some of the heroes were simpletons, of course, Waverley and Henry Morton and Bertram and Nigel, but they mattered very slightly. Sometimes they occupied too much space; if only that great man could return and give us three whole volumes about Dandy Dinmont and his family and nobody else at all! But I had my own resource for that, and Dinmont and Edie Ochiltree and Dalgetty and Nicol Jarvie and even Peter Peebles have histories that extend far beyond the written page.

It was with Scott, moreover, that a new and important development in my reading occurred. As I have said, I had never as yet considered the existence of the author behind the book; one's reading would perhaps be the finer if that happy state could continue to the end, if one knew nothing about Milton's patient daughters, or Byron's adventures in Italy, or Shelley's Harriet, or Keats' Fanny Brawne, or Tolstoi's escape from his domesticity, or Hugo's pomposities, or George Eliot's horse-like countenance. I don't know how this may be; in any case readers have no choice in these days of crowding personal biographies. I was lucky, I fancy, to have Scott for my first personal encounter. Somebody gave me a little, shabby, truncated Lockhart, and the excitement of that story was as intense as any of the novels. I took, of course, furiously Scott's side, I could have wrung the necks of the Ballantynes, and when a little later I read the two volumes of the JOURNAL (enough for Scott's immortal fame had there never been any novels) his tragic crisis was so vivid to me that for weeks afterwards it was as though my closest friend had lost his money, his wife and his health in one overwhelming catastrophe, and I powerless to assist him. But best of all, of course, were those earlier days of prosperity, the grand house rising so magnificent above the Tweed, guests, Kings and Princes, the finest writers in England,

the most enchanting ladies coming in a
fine crowd to pay their homage; and then,
best touch of all, the Ettrick shepherd or
Tom Purdie having a crack with their
friend as though there had never been
any fine people there at all.

At any rate, for good or for ill, I knew
what I wanted now, both from life and
from reading.

So far novels and romances had been my
only food. Reading must be a personal
adventure or the salt goes out of it, and
any acquaintance with poetry that I had
was thrust on me from outside, either in
the forced learning of Wordsworth or
Campbell in dreary hours at school or in
the superior remarks of some elder: "I
can't think why you must be forever
reading stories when there are so many
better things. . . ."

Well, I wasn't going to be driven into
it that way, but, of course, as though the
patron saint of all readers has his eye
eternally alert, the right moment came in
the only possible way.

I was staying with an uncle at Canter-
bury for the Christmas holidays; it was

27

a snowy afternoon and, going by chance
into a bookshop, I found three thick little
books in a binding new to me, the first
volumes, I was told, of a wonderful new
series. They were cheap, they were thick,
they were seductive; the series was named
THE WORLD'S CLASSICS, and the three
volumes that I then purchased and took
home with me were Hazlitt's ESSAYS, Poe's
TALES and POEMS by KEATS. I went back
to the warm, thickly curtained library and
sat over the fire. My uncle's house
abutted on the Cathedral, and as I read
the organ was rumbling and humming as
though it were in the very room with me.
Although I could not see it, I knew that
the snow was falling thickly beyond the
windows; in the next room they were hanging holly over the pictures. I think almost
any book in the world would have been
entrancing to me that afternoon, but when
I began ON GOING A JOURNEY and passed
from that to THE INDIAN JUGGLERS I
knew a richness of satisfaction that was
quite astounding in its surprise. I read
on and on and then, passing from one
thick volume to the other, began:

Deep in the shady sadness of a vale
Far sunken from the healthy breath of morn,
Far from the fiery noon, and eve's one star,
Sat grey-hair'd Saturn, quiet as a stone,
Still as the silence round about his lair;
Forest on forest hung about his head
Like cloud on cloud.   No stir of air was
       there,
Not so much life as on a summer's day
Robs not one light seed from the feather'd
       grass,
But where the dead leaf fell, there did it rest.
A stream went voiceless by, still deaden'd
       more
By reason of his fallen divinity
Spreading a shade: the Naïad 'mid her reeds
Press'd her cold finger closer to her lips.

Then I knew that something magical
had indeed happened to me and that life
would now be twice as rich as ever it had
been before but that the period of Reading
for Fun was over.

CHAPTER TWO

READING FOR EDUCATION

OF all the snobberies common to man the literary variation is, I think, the least harmful. That is, I suppose, because it is really based on a love of beautiful things, yet a great many very fine and handsome readers are quite innocent of it. I divided, at the beginning of my Essay, nursery readers into the two grand divisions of Romantics and Realists, and now the time has come for a later division into the two great nationalities of the Sophisticated and the Unsophisticated, and one of the principal characteristics of the Sophisticated is that they have been all at one time or another literary snobs.

I like to think of the Unsophisticated; charming and happy creatures, they are seeking only to gratify their simple and sensuous emotions, passing from the two-

pence-coloured pamphlets through the
swashbuckling romances of the great
Dumas or the happy family chronicles of
the author of THE HEIR OF REDCLIFFE,
or the poetry of Mrs. Hemans, Longfellow
and Sir Edwin Arnold to the mature, uncritical happiness of anything that seems
to them real and true and beautiful. It
is the fashion in the more superior literary
journals of our time to sneer at the Unsophisticated; almost nothing is done for
their reading by these journals. Because
they are moved by Longfellow as well as
by Tennyson, by Mrs. Humphry Ward
equally with Jane Austen, by the latest
successful novel of the day and by Mr.
De La Mare's fairy stories at one and
the same time, therefore little articles are
written making fun of them, sarcastic
poems are composed in their honour by
very clever young poets, and the true love
of literature is said to be quite beyond
their experience.

But is it? Because the Unsophisticated
have never considered whether their reading is good form or no is merely an argu-
ment in favour of their honesty; the Unsophisticated indeed have no opportunity

of being anything but honest. There are times perhaps when they are shy of their appreciation, when some very clever relation has raised an eyebrow at their enthusiasms or some young critic has been entertained at dinner and has listened to them with that superior tolerance that is so natural an attitude for young critics. They blush then a little, they hedge a trifle perhaps, they try hurriedly to summon to their memories any works with fine-sounding titles that have given them pleasure, but their innocent attempts at such snobbery are happily short-lived, their true enthusiasms will keep breaking through, and it is no more possible for them to disown their favourites than it is for Mr. Walkley, say, to pretend an ignorance of the works of Aristophanes or Marcel Proust.

How different are the Sophisticated! I would not for a moment deny them their virtues; it may well be that it is in their hands that the true growth of literature lies, for they are the ones ever on the lookout for the latest superior thing, and as the latest superior thing will almost certainly sell very few copies indeed it is the

Sophisticated alone who are able to nourish its life and keep it fed and housed until the wide world is ready to recognize its importance.

The Reading of the very young Sophisticated, however, is not as a rule concerned with contemporary genius. He must first be fed on all the earlier superior works, and it is at this stage in his Reading that the temptation to snobbery will attack him most severely. The youthful Reader of seventeen or eighteen, when he first sniffs the delightful airs of fine writing, will discover immediately that he is different from many of his companions. I had only to taste Hazlitt, Keats, and some of the Elizabethan dramatists to find that I was considered by some of my contemporaries to be a rather superior person. This had never occurred to me before; indeed during my reading of Scott and some of the early nineteenth-century novelists I was thought to be rather stupid and sadly behind the times, but I found that for some mysterious reason my liking for Hazlitt's Essays and Lamb's Letters and yet more my rather nightmarish

pleasure in the plays of Webster and Ford
moved me into another world. I was im-
mensely pleased by this; I had always
thought myself rather unusual, and had
never quite understood why it was that I
was not more generally considered so. A
new subtle element crept into my Reading;
I enjoyed Hazlitt and Lamb, of course,
that first thrill on that Christmas evening had been far too authentic to be
doubted, but I began now to read under
the observation of others, and I began,
worst of all, to read things because they
were difficult, and to fancy that I understood them when most assuredly I did not.

Every generation provides for its
literary young its own especially difficult
tests; to-day it may be that the poems of
Doughty or Mr. T. S. Eliot are the particular temptations; twenty years ago
SORDELLO and the novels of Meredith were
still fresh enough to serve that purpose.
SORDELLO I read while I was still at school
from beginning to end, and I did, I think,
obtain a sort of confused pleasure from
it. Fine words stuck out like plums in a
pudding here and there; I had a glorious

picture in my mind of an Italian night piece with rude battlements and towers, fires flashing, the clashing of arms in the invisible dark and Sordello himself somewhere singing his songs. If I had been content with that no harm was done, but I pretended to myself as well as to others that I understood every word of it, and I am still able to blush at the recollection of an unhappy evening when an old fierce professor of my father's college produced a page of it and challenged me to interpret!

But the devil of this business is that once falseness has crept in there is no stopping it. A true Reader, that is, one to whom books are like bottles of whiskey to the inebriate, to whom anything that is between covers has a sort of intoxicating savour, is unable often to distinguish between that same love of a book as a book and the real grasping of it as an individual creation. In some mysterious fashion all books that were considered æsthetically superior had from that very consideration a fascinating shape and colour. I remember that I carried about

with me at this time an old volume of
Landor's GEBIR, only because I had understood that it was something that almost
nobody had read and that it was only
appreciated by the very finest spirits. Yes,
I carried it about with me, but at this
time did not read a word of it, always
intending to, loving to see it there lying
on my table like some mysterious orchid,
and loving it especially when some one
picked it up, examined it and wondered
that I could be so wise.

These are lamentable confessions, but I
suspect that most readers have one day or
another known something of the kind, and
after all who can tell but that there may
not be something not quite dishonourable
about it; who knows but that the books
themselves are not working actively in the
matter? SORDELLO, it is true, I have never
quite heartily liked, too much manner and
too little matter perhaps, something of
literary snobbishness on Browning's own
part somewhere, but GEBIR had not to
wait so very long before my affectation
changed into something most truthful and
sincere. Do you remember:

Now disappear the Liparean isles
Behind, and forward hang the Etrurian
    coasts,
Verdant with privet and with juniper.
Now faith is plighted: piled on every hearth,
Crackle the consecrated branches, heard
Propitious, and from vases rough embost
Through the light ember falls the bubbling
    wine
And now the chariot of the sun descends!
The waves rush hurried from the foaming
    steeds:
Smoke issues from their nostrils at the gate;
Which, when we enter, with huge golden bar
Atlas and Calpe close across the main.

The final lure for my snobbery, however,
was nothing so innocent as GEBIR, but
rather the overwhelming personality and
power of George Meredith. Every literary
age has, of course, its own especial
fetiches; the fetich of to-day, I fancy, is
the poetry of Thomas Hardy, and there
is, I am sure, many a young snob at
Oxford and Cambridge at this particular
moment who, just as the mediæval hermit
forced himself into his hair shirt, is driving
into his young consciousness a determined
admiration for those marvellously crabbed

and gnarled poems. Meredith's novels twenty years ago were far from being remote as in so many ways they are to-day. He was unpopular, he was a rebel, he was a creator of glorious women, he wrote in a difficult and richly-tangled prose. One of the unquestioned results of the European war is that we are turning more and more towards honest simplicity in our Reading. Defoe and Swift and Jane Austen, John Clare and Barnes and their kind, are now our heroes and heroines, and I venture to prophesy that the young author of LADY INTO FOX will prove to be the ancestor of many a tale almost as simple if not quite as innocent as THE FAIRCHILD FAMILY. But twenty years ago we were still caught in the web of all the fine affectations of the 'nineties, and at Cambridge, at least, it was still unaffected to believe nakedly in affectation.

I certainly had no consciousness that my Meredithian fervour was insincere. It began quite definitely on a fine summer's afternoon in Cambridge when my father and mother, sitting under a hedge in a field, read THE EGOIST, the one to the other. I, near at hand, heard my father

consider Meredith's "difficulty," and from
that moment I was caught. It is quite
true to say that THE EGOIST won me to
a new conception of the possibilities of
fiction. The novels hitherto known to me
had been concerned in the main with external action, and although that action
might not be very important, as, for instance, in the stories of Jane Austen, when
the principal excitement was a ball in the
Bath Assembly Rooms or the expectation
of a proposal of marriage, nevertheless
the characters moved, there was changing
background, people were clothed in definite
costumes. Now in THE EGOIST nothing
external was of importance compared with
the manœuvres of heart and soul. It is
true that Clara Middleton attempted to
run away, that Doctor Middleton enjoyed
his wine, and that in Crossjay there was a
real living kicking schoolboy, but no physical movement compared for excitement
with the spiritual state of the characters;
Sir Willoughby was the thing, and as his
soul was revealed to you it was like a
bird's-eye view of a new and marvellous
country. This book I loved and with, I
think, a true appreciation of what was

grand in it, but I can see now on looking
back that there was a terrible deal of
unreality about my passion for some of
the others. Oddly enough, the one that I
cared for most truly after THE EGOIST
was the most difficult of all, ONE OF OUR
CONQUERORS, and I shall always think until I die the heroine of that book the
princess of English beauties. EVAN HAR-
RINGTON entertained me, and the first half
of THE AMAZING MARRIAGE will have for
me always a strange mountainous haunt-
ing beauty lovely in its dim retrospect. But
HARRY RICHMOND and VITTORIA and THE
TRAGIC COMEDIAN, and even the famous
DIANA herself, were difficult work; I never
really believed in them, and I fought my
way through their pages like Jabberwock
in his forest. But did I honestly say so?
No, alas! I did not; I made it my test
of everyone I met as to whether they read
Meredith or no, and if they did not my
eyebrows went up in a surprised distress,
and I hurriedly but pointedly and a little
pityingly turned the conversation into
other directions. There were at the same
time other servants of my affectation;
Walter Pater was one of them, Francis

Thompson a second, Beddoes a third. Pater, fifteen years later, I was to recapture with a fresh sense of delighted discovery, although even now I feel that there is inside him a cool green slab of marble, such as Browning's Bishop ordered for his tomb, instead of a heart. 1 have yet a notebook filled with my literary dicta of that time, extracts from DEATH'S JEST BOOK are scattered like freckles all over the paper, and I write about THE HOUND OF HEAVEN as though I were in truth Thompson's one worthy reader. I had a very small library at this time, but my fine poets and dramatists, my superior essayists and one or two French novels (the last almost entirely unintelligible to me) were arranged ostentatiously upon my shelves; I was always vexed did anyone come into my room and not notice them.

I was saved from hopeless ruin by the intrusion of Carlyle and by a sudden panic-driven suspicion that I was completely uneducated. I wonder how many readers in his own good time Carlyle has thus saved, and I wonder, too, at what stage in life as a rule the idle lotus-eating

reader has been conscious of this sudden
thirst for education.

We are told constantly about the many
serious people who from their earliest
years read only for education. They begin apparently with Mrs. Taylor's CAU-
TIONARY TALES, pass on through LIVES
OF THE SAINTS into a full enjoyment of
the Classics, thence slide gently into Kant
and Schopenhauer, disport themselves
freely among comparative religions and,
at the age of twenty-one, are fine, tabulat-
ing, reasoning creatures about whom
there is no nonsense and for whom nothing in life holds a mystery. And indeed
the last thing that I intend to do is to
sneer. I have never known what it is to
be a student of anything, I have never
had the clear-headedness, the application,
the austerity of life, and, moreover, it is
absurd to pretend, as I have seen men do,
that it is impossible to obtain fine ecstasy
from the works of Kant and Schopenhauer
and the intricate conclusions of Bergson
and Einstein. I incline my head before
brains of such calibre, and we all know
that it is the most learned philosophers

and mathematicians who delight in fairy stories and detective tales.

The difficulty is that to be deliberately self-educative limits sadly one's unself-consciousness. As soon as I discovered that I ought to be better educated I began priggishly to consider what would be the books that would educate me best, and that deliberation hindered, deny it as I might, my innocent pleasure.

There were, for instance, the Classics. I had learnt, like most English public schoolboys at that time, nothing at all at school. I had spent week after week over the parsing of ten lines of Euripides or Virgil, I had been kept in for many a sunny afternoon because of the wrong placing of a Greek accent, I had constructed with infinite difficulty some of the worst Latin verses known to man, but no single human soul during all those eight years at school had given me any sense at all of the glowing excitement of Homer, the quiet pastoral beauty of Virgil, or the human drama of Euripides. I was to discover Homer years later from Chapman, and Euripides from Gilbert Murray, and Æschylus from the Loeb Library, but at this time the whole classical world was a dim, mist-shadowed country surrounded with a kind of Chinese wall of impossible grammar and long accent-haunted sentences. Of Philosophy I knew nothing at all, of History only some sensational episodes, and of foreign languages enough to translate a page of TARTARIN with difficult inaccuracy, and a scene of Schiller into stiff, lop-sided sentences.

It is perhaps worth while to pause here for a moment and consider a specimen of the perfectly educated Reader, partly because in any discourse on Reading he assuredly deserves a place, and partly because it is only just that I should present a type so far away from my own. A——— W——— (I know that if he sees this and recognises himself he will forgive me) must from the very earliest age have been a perfect specimen of the Educated Reader. He always loved books and truly loved them, but never allowed himself any heady enthusiasm about them. I did not know him as a boy, but I am sure that whether it was Henty or Baines Read or Hans Andersen that he was reading he read like a little spider sitting in the centre of his web and waiting for the right fly to come to him. He must have always had that gift for exactly extracting from his material the essential food for his precise need. On Henty he would nourish his desire for facts, with Hans Andersen and Grimm he would encourage his need for the fantastic, with Baines Read he would study that queer thing Boy.

It was a classical mind that he really had, but he knew something about mathematics and chemistry, modern languages and the literature of sport, and from all these he gathered just enough and no more. If his real love was for classical literature he very soon became aware that it would not be truly educative to permit its fascination to enchant him too completely. He went through Eton and Oxford, I believe, as a most brilliant classical scholar, but he would always make it his business to talk to the men whom he met on their subjects and not on his own in order that he might never pass an hour that should not inform him about something. When I first met him I was still in my heady condition of admiring only the best literature. I remember during the

first evening that we spent together his
polite interest in my Swinburne and Ros-
setti enthusiasms, and indeed he was so
kind and attentive that I soon passed to
my genuine love for Scott and the early
nineteenth-century novelists and essayists.
You might have thought to listen to him
that he had never read a line of anything,
and that for the first time in his life it
occurred to him that it was very important that he should know more about the
Waverley novels and Hazlitt and Lamb.
He listened to me most deferentially, and
when at last I ventured to say something
about Greek literature he waved me at once
away as though that were a subject in
which he had not the slightest interest.

It was only afterwards, when I visited
his astonishing and marvellously arranged
library and heard from others of his astounding universal erudition, that I
blushed for my self-confident *naïveté*. How,
I thought, he must have mocked at me in
private, how childish and ignorant he
must have considered me. But there I
believe that I did him an injustice; he
may well have been amazed at my confused
and ill-ordered mind, but he probably in

the course of the evening acquired one or two facts that were useful to him about Walter Scott, and although he had, I think, no more than the average amount of self-conceit, he was so well accustomed to finding every brain disordered and ignorant in comparison with his own that I was for him no novelty.

He was an extreme and brilliant example of the kind of Reader concerning whose merits I can never quite make up my mind. One sees them everywhere, notebook in pocket, furrowed brow and a sort of Extension-Lecture attitude to the world. It is the Reader of this sort who underlines with thick pencil marks the books that he reads, and comments down the side of the page on misprints, topographical inaccuracies and foolish philosophies. I am a little prejudiced against this kind, I think, because he is the terror of the novelist, is forever writing letters to say that the moon has risen on some occasion when it should not, and that it would be impossible for the hero to arrive by such and such a train from such and such a place. I once, I remember, received fifty or sixty letters pointing out that a lady in one of my novels has a moustache on one page and none at all on another, and I was blamed from many quarters of the country on another occasion because my hero resident in Cornwall read the *Morning Post* at breakfast.

The danger of being too thoroughly educated in your reading is that education becomes with you a vice, you dare not read anything by chance lest you should be wasting the time over a poor book that you ought to be giving to a good one. It is very hard too if you are a really educated Reader to avoid an attitude of superiority to all other Readers. Educated critics are, I think, the worst of all in this; of course you may have so lively a fancy for the foibles of human nature that, as with Sir Edmund Gosse, for instance, your educated pages are everywhere enlightened with human observations, or you may, like Mr. A. C. Bradley, be a genius of your kind and so above all human laws. But the ordinary educated critic is often a nuisance both to writers and to readers because his own education is of so much more importance to him than the glorious excitement of literature.

When I discovered the horrible facts about my own lack of education I hurried tumultuously, as many another Reader has done, to improve myself. I laid down a schedule of daily reading, I determined that no more works of fiction should lie in my hands for years to come save possibly on Sundays, for an hour before breakfast I would read the Classics, in the morning when my regular University work was over I would study philosophy, in the evening modern languages should be my delight. The difficulty about the Classics, I soon discovered, was that I was still in the stage of Fourth Form knowledge, that is, I could translate with the aid of a dictionary at the rate of about ten lines an hour. The natural sequence of this was that I was an easy prey to cribs; cribs of the superior kind were in fact so fascinating that the original Greek and Latin were soon left far behind, and it did not seem necessary to go back and pick them up again when one knew so exactly what it was that they were trying to say.

The trouble with the philosophy, on the other hand, was that it was either so simple as to seem childish, or so difficult as to be unintelligible. Philosophy needed, I discovered, a particular absorption of mind that was not apparently mine. When I had read a page or two of Hegel, we will say, my thoughts began to wander so destructively that I had to begin from the beginning again. Nietzsche seemed to me comparatively straightforward, but then I did not believe in anything that he said. And that was a further difficulty. When I had understood a little of the philosophy presented to me, my own natural philosophy, although obviously jejune and childish, was the only one that appeared to answer my particular case. My stature was simply not tall enough for these fine overwhelming systems, and I felt as I always feel in the Swiss mountains, that my own English lakes are really more my own size.

With the modern languages my education was a little more satisfactory. If my memory is clear I made a miraculous leap from the painful line-by-line elucida-

tion of my school TARTARIN into the very
arms of Balzac himself. It seems incredible, but I believe that quite suddenly and
as it were by a sort of divine dispensation
I had a clear understanding of the by no
means uncomplicated finances of that
citizen of Paris. I don't know how it happened, I have never, as a matter of fact,
been able to read any other French quite
so easily as the French of Balzac; his
French is, I believe, not difficult, although
clumsy and cumbrous; I only know that
when I read Balzac in translation I do
not feel that I am gaining anything or
that I have missed very much of the
French, whereas when I read Mr. Scott
Moncrieff's marvellous translation of
Proust I realize that in the original I
simply understood nothing at all. In any
case, with this discovery that I could
understand Balzac there came a great leap
forward in my educational reading; snobbery again, I suppose, and I must confess
that at this distance of time it is very
difficult to dissever the pride in my understanding any language whatever in its
original from the real happiness that I

caught from the art of the books that I was reading.

But how many Readers really love the literature of a foreign country, whatever they may pretend? Certain great writers —Goethe, Dostoievsky, Balzac, Cervantes, Dante, Tolstoi—become by a kind of gigantic simplicity world voices, and no one may flatter himself with any especial credit for catching at least an echo of their intention. But this other business of understanding the literature of another country better than your own, that must surely in all sincerity be very rare. With painting and music, of course not; many a minor French painter has captured beauty for all the world to see, and music is surely a universal language. But when we come to this intricate twisting, elusive tangle of words life is not nearly long enough for the beginning of knowledge of our own. In that very strangeness of a foreign tongue there lurks, I suppose, magic, and I can remember that the first time that I heard some one in Moscow recite a poem of Pushkin's I was enchanted. But I was enchanted by the power of music only, whereas when I read TINTERN ABBEY or THE ODE TO THE SKYLARK, or THE SCHOLAR GIPSY or Crashaw's FLAMING HEART, I have the music and then beyond that the contact with the soul, intellectual, physical and spiritual, of the artist.

Even the most perfect translation wins you only halfway. The most perfect translations in my time in English have been Constance Garnett's editions of Tolstoi, Turgeniev and Tchekhov, and Scott Moncrieff's Marcel Proust, to which I have already alluded. How marvellous Mrs. Garnett's translation of Dostoievsky is anyone who has the slightest knowledge of the original will eagerly recognise, but inevitably so much, so very much, is lost by the mere sound of the words. Her translation of WAR AND PEACE is a masterpiece, but VOENA E MIR and then WAR AND PEACE—does not the title drop in translation into a world of flattened intensity? So that it is, I fancy, a few great masters alone who push triumphantly over their country's surroundings, and even there, fate is so strange, it is still credibly held on the Continent, I believe, that our greatest three writers are Shakespeare, Byron and Oscar Wilde, with Dickens a languishing fourth and Thackeray and Fielding nowhere at all, and one has only to talk to an educated Frenchman or Russian to discover an astonishment that we consider Thomas Hardy one of our finest novelists.

I suspect then that for most of us, if we are honest, our foreign reading is pursued mainly because it is educational and not because we love it. French novels were a good deal read, I fancy, in the 'nineties in England because of their salacity, by ladies upon whose hands time hung heavily, but of course that could be so no longer in this our day, when our own novels go so beautifully far in that direction.

But the education demon, when he has once poked his nose into our reading, never quite leaves us again; it is he who finally once and forever has driven us out of that Elysian garden where once we read only for fun. I have in front of me now a little yellow-coloured paper upon which twenty years ago I wrote these serious words:—

READING

TO BE READ BEFORE THE END OF MARCH

Pater . . . . "The Renaissance."
"Marius the Epicurean."
Carlyle . . . "Frederick the Great."
"Past and Present."
"Oliver Cromwell."
Nietzsche . . "Thus Spake Zarathustra."
Bury . . . . "Mediæval History."
Zola . . . . . "La Terre."
"Paris."
Wilberforce . . Sermons (six volumes).
Beowulf
Calderon . . . Plays.
Stendhal . . . "Le Rouge et le Noir."

What a touching and admirable list this
is! How moving the insertion of LA
TERRE into the middle of it, how wide
and admirable a field it covers! But the
pale spectre of Duty hanging over it rids
it of all its charm. History especially
suffered from my stern educational prin-
ciples—History that should be the most
glorious, captivating and moving of all
the written arts after Poetry, and yet
apparently the most difficult of all to
achieve successfully. I was reading during these years for honours in History
and was rewarded at the last with the

fine distinction of obtaining no marks at
all in the Ancient History paper, and that
was partly, I remember, because we had
to study among many other things the
details of Napoleon's 1814 campaign. As
the lean kine swallowed up the fat in the
Bible so did the minutiæ of these months
in Napoleon's career swallow up all the
rest of my historical studies. We had to
follow from day to day and even from
hour to hour every movement in that
wonderful drama, every road and every
village became vivid to me, military orders
and private letters, unimportant officials,
details of dress, colds and coughs and
sudden headaches, here was a world into
which I could plunge myself with understanding. But these other arrays of dates
and national movements and successions
of kings and princes, it was all the mere
scaffolding of life to me. One short
hour in the career of Pericles, could I
have truly perceived it, meant more to
me than all the struggles of Sparta. No,
it was of no use to make me educational,
I simply had neither the brain nor the
patience.

My final vision of myself during this

strenuous time of progress is not a splendid one. I am a schoolmaster, by what whim of fate who can tell? Rows of tousel-headed boys are waiting for a lesson in French grammar, and now I begin: "This morning I will tell you a story and you will deliver up to me next lesson a translation of this in your best French—'A few years ago, on a dark and windy evening in Paris, a tall man, his face hidden in a black coat, might be observed passing swiftly down a side street'———."

Yes, very sad. I was a schoolmaster for the merest year; education with me had sadly failed.

READING FOR LOVE

AND so at last one has learnt how to read, only for oneself, of course. What one has truly learnt perhaps, if honesty is the only wear, is that one will never for the rest of one's days become a Reader of the finest class, never one of those splendid persons who are orderly, systematic and philosophical, and never one, I suspect, with that fine impeccable taste that can sift at once the chaff from the wheat or perform an instant judicial separation between the sheep and the goats.

"See a person's books and you know what a kind of person that is." Very true; see a man's library and you know where his heart is, if he has a heart. See a man's library . . . Yes, now at last I have reached the warm comfortable corner of my Essay.

I have seen so many libraries in my time that I am perhaps a little confused about them, but the noblest library I have ever seen is the grand one in Boston, and the friendliest the Morgan library in New York, and the most interesting Mr. Thomas Wise's library in Hampstead, and the most touching a certain farmer's library here in Cumberland, and the stupidest and most dead a millionaire's library in—well, never mind where, and the bravest library the Braille Library in London, and the most accommodating library the London Library itself, and the smallest library the library of the Queen's Doll's House, and the most depressing library any circulating library of fiction anywhere, and the dullest library the library of a clerical acquaintance of mine in Rutlandshire, and the most delightful, best-arranged, happiest-looking, heart-warming library my own in—again, never mind where.

The worst libraries, of course, and the only ones to be firmly excluded from this part of my essay are those accursed things in glazed sets behind glass. It is as hard for love of books to enter into such a library as it is for the familiar camel to pass through the well-known eye of a needle; it *can* be done if only the sets are ancient enough and shabby enough, but the best friend I have among booksellers, Mr. James Bain of King William Street, told me once of an order some one had to supply a rich gentleman's house with a library, and the only point of importance about the books chosen was that they should be formed of a certain size so as to fill the proper spaces in the bookshelves neatly.

Libraries should be penetrated with the love of books, so that when you enter a room where the books are the air is warm with a kind of delicious humanity, and the books have been always so affectionately treated that, like the right kind of dog, they know no fear and yet have their fitting dignity.

There is no rule as to the proper contents of a library, only it must be personal to its owner. You can, like Mr. John Burns, have a library all about London, or you may, like Sir Edmund Gosse, have a passion for the Elizabethan and Restoration drama, or you may, like my friend Aristides, care only for books about mountaineering, but what you must be is honest to the impulses of your heart. That brings one, of course, to the vexed question of Collecting and the fascinating tyranny of First Editions. There is no question so hotly debated among book lovers as this; only yesterday one of the truest lovers of books said to me that he could see nothing in old editions, and all that he wanted was a fine clear type and an impeccable text.

I can speak, I think, with some knowledge on this subject, because the First Edition fever entered my blood at a certain quite definite moment and left it again at another, so that I am free of it now and can look upon the disease with a dispassionate eye. That does not mean that I would for a moment surrender the original editions that I possess; I love them all, and I think that they have a certain affection in return for me; but the passion is over, I haunt the splendid halls of Hodgson and Sotheby no longer, Mr. Maggs and Mr. Quaritch send me their magnificent catalogues now in vain (I would not have them cease to do this;

61

one never knows when one may begin again).

I caught the disease late. It was in the War, when I was home on leave from Russia and attended one of those magnificent Red Cross sales with a friend; the first edition of THE MONK by Mr. Matthew Lewis was held up to us, and my friend said: "Would you like to have that?" and I said "Yes," and began to nod to the auctioneer's bid. I nodded as far as my purse would allow me and then with a sigh retired, only to be amazed by hearing my friend say to me a moment later: "You've got them, they're yours," and then found that he also for my sake had been nodding, and that we two had been the only bidders in the room.

This somewhat irritating initiation was my undoing. For the next five years I haunted every old bookshop in England. I bought, of course, at first unwisely, but soon learnt a thing or two, and hardest lesson of all, trained myself to fit my desires to my purse. Never for me the Kilmarnock Burns and Gray's ELEGY and a second Folio, but there are plenty of things easier than those, and, indeed, when